John C. Nolan
xii 1962.

TOULOUSE-LAUTREC

TOULOUSE-LAUTREC

By PAUL DE LAPPARENT
Translated by W. F. H. WHITMARSH
With forty illustrations

LONDON
JOHN LANE THE BODLEY HEAD LIMITED
1928

*Made and printed in France by
Les Éditions Rieder, 7, place Saint-
Sulpice, Paris.*

LIST OF PLATES[1]

(1) The photographs of the works reproduced in this volume were obtained from the following sources : Plates no. 1, 3, 4, 10, 11, 12, 13, 14, 18, 19, 20, 21, 22, 23, 25, from the Maison Aillaud, Albi ; Plates no. 5, 7, 9, from the Ateliers Druet ; Plates no. 2, 8, 17, 24, 26 to 40, from the Archives Photographiques ; Plate no. 15, from the Maison Laffont, Toulouse ; Plate no. 6 is reproduced from a photograph by Joyant ; Plate no. 16 is reproduced from a photographic negative in the possession of Mme Pierre Decourcelle.

TOULOUSE-LAUTREC

I N the heyday of Impressionism, at the time when Claude Monet, Sisley, Pissarro and so many others were setting up their easels in the open air and expressing in their pictures the mellow sunshine on the fields, there was one painter who, though he professed to share their theories, dwelt in a quiet retreat in the shade of the city, at Montmartre, and from this observatory studied the passers-by : not the light which illumined them, but rather their features and expressions, especially those revealing character.

At such a time, this painter seems an anomaly. It is true he could not roam the countryside in search of subjects : his withered legs made such exercise impossible.

Henri de Toulouse-Lautrec-Monfa was born at Albi on November 24, 1864 of the marriage of first cousins, Alphonse de Toulouse-Lautrec-Monfa and Adèle Tapié de Celeyran. He was descended from the Counts of Toulouse who once ruled over the Albigeois region, several of whom married princesses of royal blood. Whether warriors or hunters, his ancestors had been essentially men of action. He would have dearly loved to follow their pursuits and emulate his father, who was a fine horseman and one of the last experts in falconry. Unfortunately his health was very poor and he had peculiarly fragile bones.

At the various residences of his family, at Albi, the Château du Bosc (near Albi), the Château de Malromé (near Bordeaux), Celeyran (near Narbonne), he began his studies under the supervision of his mother, who was a woman of culture and had a sound knowledge of Latin.

In 1872, his father, wishing to move nearer the Orléanais district, where he had sporting estates, settled in Paris and sent the boy to the Lycée Fontanes.

The family took a house with studio attached in the Cité du Retiro (at the corner of the Faubourg Saint-Honoré and the Rue Boissy d'Anglas). In the studio Count de Toulouse-Lautrec did modelling and bred a variety of animals. Every morning he went out riding. As he wished to breakfast in the Bois de Boulogne, he took to riding a milch mare. Close by the Cascade, he would produce a cup, milk his mare, settle himself under a tree and sop a bread-roll in the milk...

But the Count, far from being a rediculous figure, was really a gentleman of fine bearing. His son portrays him (Plate xxvi) as erect, head aloft, brushing his thick beard with so sculptural a gesture that you cannot help exclaiming : « A Rude (1), a veritable Rude ! »

Lautrec senior was no fool. He was a great sportsman, but there was also much of the artist in him. He once rented some shooting water in the Sologne region. On one occasion, when he was entertaining one of his friends, just as the latter was bringing his gun up to fire, the Count called out : « Just a moment ! Don't shoot, please ! You might frighten the birds and they would never come back again, and I am so fond of seeing them fly over these pools. »

---

(1) François Rude, celebrated French sculptor (1784-1855). — Translator's note.

The father's eccentricity accounts largely for the son's but it cannot be taken as proving lack of intellect.

In July 1874, the boy carried off a number of prizes. Circumstances, however, were against him. His parents could never seem to settle in one place. They moved house, first from Paris into Orléanais, thence into Narbonnais, to Nice, to the Château de Malromé and then to Albi. Eventually Henri had to be withdrawn from the Lycée altogether. Moreover, his poor health necessitated a stay at Amélie-les-Bains, where he was given treatment.

His bones grew no firmer and at Albi, in 1878, he slipped on a polished floor and broke his thigh. He was taken away to Barèges, and there, in the following year, he fell into a dry torrent gully, and the other thigh was broken! His mother rushed for a doctor, leaving the boy sitting on the ground, supporting his leg with both hands to prevent the bones from moving, and he waited in this position without a tear or a complaint.

The fractured bones set badly and his legs stopped growing. But, in these years, his mind opened out and his memory stored up countless impressions.

The various periods he spent in the country, far from giving him pleasure, only served to sharpen his disappointment. He used to see his cousins set out with the huntsmen and dogs, and could not go with them. In these galling moments he would take his pencil and draw with furious energy.

He had received some advice from one of his father's friends, the animal painter Princeteau. In Paris he often went with this artist to circuses and to the Jardin des Plantes to observe and sketch. He had also watched his father modelling statuettes of horses and dogs. His uncle Charles de Toulouse-Lautrec, his boon friend and correspondent, was also a devotee of art and did some painting.

Pascal has said that men are unhappy because they cannot

keep their room in peace. They must be off to the wars, or
they must undertake some journey. They cannot stay indoors
and meditate.

Toulouse-Lautrec owed something to his infirmity, in that
he did not waste his attention in unprofitable directions.

His disappointment bred in him a strong dislike of the
country and a contempt for landscape. That is why he confined his interest to living creatures.

It was plain that painting was his vocation. In early
childhood he used to cover the margins and blank spaces of
his copy-books with little drawings. Even at the age of three,
he shewed this innate love of drawing. After a baptism, as the
family was going into the vestry to sign the register, he said :
« I want to sign too. » — « But you can't write yet, child. » —
« Very well, I will draw an ox ! »

So there was no reason for surprise when he resolved to
devote himself entirely to art.

No matter ! When a son decides on such a vocation, it
comes as a shock to a family of « good social standing ». It is
no career. — He will have affairs with models ! If he wants to
marry, what family will recognise him? That is how people
of « high social status » thought at the end of last century.

It must be admitted that in Lautrec's case several of these
objections did not count. For him, the artist's calling was, if
not a career (for after all what career could he have followed?),
at least an occupation. — Besides, there was no need for him
to earn a living, and marriage was out of the question.

So it was decided that the boy should have his way. Still, it
was necessary to exercise great care. He shewed initiative,
the evidence of energy which might assert itself in extraordinary conduct, as steam and electricity provide the motive
power for dangerous machines, which though men use they
fear. Such forces have to be kept under control.

In view of these considerations, Lautrec's parents made

him take lessons with a recognised master. He started in Bonnat's studio in 1882.

It is quite legitimate to make painters learn their craft thoroughly. On pain of encountering a thousand obstacles, they must know which colours are durable, and which of these choice materials may be mixed without fear of the chemical reactions which would in time alter the tint. Again, they must know the tones which shew up brighter when associated. And then there are the laws of perspective! If the artist has not a thorough knowledge of these, the mistakes he will continually be making will take all sense of reality out of his compositions. A painter who left the Beaux-Arts with such technical equipment, that is to say with a sound knowledge of chemistry, optics and geometry, like a good student of higher mathematics, would not fail to put on his pictures the letters which qualified architects cut on the houses they build : D. P. L. G.

In 1887 Bonnat gave up his studio, and Lautrec went on to Cormon's, where he only stayed a short time.

It is a far cry from the leisurely art of a plodding, conscientious painter who has chosen his calling and career with a view to earning a living and filling in his time, to the tyrannical, possessing Art of the man who everywhere, at all times, keeps drawing with tireless energy, watching for movements and gestures, delving into characters, classifying his discoveries and adding them to a monument of Art which year by year grows more complete, more ornate and perfect.

Denied the long rambles of the landscape painter, and indeed having no taste for landscape, he was to develop a passion for the study of the human body. What he wanted was not the studio nude, as he had seen it at Bonnat's and Cormon's, but the nude in motion. His special function was to watch the play of muscles and the expressions of faces. His representation of life came direct from the actual life of his models, his pencil moving as they moved.

Gestures are the manifestations of some inner force seeking to expend itself. The gesture of a hand holding a pencil is a thing of immense significance, for how much it reveals of the intimate nature of the artist! When, for example, Watteau traces the harmonious curve of a cheek, a waist, or a calf, the line is full of tenderness and melancholy. When a writer wishes to tell us all about himself, he needs three hundred pages; but a mere sweep of the pencil and the artist stands revealed.

A gesture! How significant is even the most commonplace and least intellectual!

Watch the people sitting in a restaurant : the way in which they use their fork or raise their glass to their lips will show you immediately their breeding and habits.

Gestures may disclose not only mentality, or permanent state, but also momentary state. Imagine, for example, a graceful girl walking along the beach! She bears her head high and holds her leg straight and firm. Her step is elastic. You can see that she could ride a horse, dance, skate, wield the tennis racket, the foil or the sword. What she is using at the present moment is her leg. It is full of the suggestion of the joys of sport. You can tell she has reserves of strength. In her carriage there is verve and style... In a word, her walk reveals her state of mind. She discloses it unknowingly.

Or here is a labourer leaving the yard in the evening. With his work-bag slung over his shoulder, he lurches along over the rubble. His walk clearly expresses exhaustion. He is well nigh dropping with fatigue. Along this same rough path there steals a supple, powerful feline, ready to spring.

Toulouse-Lautrec wields a pencil, the point of which becomes his particular instrument of expression, as he follows with it the line of a shoulder or an arm.

What intense energy!

Monsieur Fourcade (1889), dressed in a frock coat, is seen

passing through a vestibule. He is hurrying. We can tell from
the forward slope of his body how rapidly he is walking.
Monsieur Louis Pascal (1893) (Plate x) pauses a moment before leaving the studio. *Miss Ida Heath* (1896) (Plate xxxvi)
stands poised on tiptoe. *Tristan Bernard at the Velodrome*
stands square and firm. All these gestures, noted down with
bold strokes, simply cry out truth. What Lautrec's weakly
body lacked, his mind had received in abundance. Some in-
ward strength, which had no power over his legs, made his
brain rich in creation. A stroke of his pencil has profound
meaning.

◨

The sculptor Devillez, standing one day before Van Dyck's
portrait etchings, remarked to me : « What fine, bold work ! »
And indeed it does require a bold eye and hand to run out
that line in the correct place on the blank sheet — the dizzy
peril of it ! — and make it convey the right suggestion of relief.
We can scarcely talk of boldness in the case of the painter
who, first of all, spreads colour over the whole canvas, and
then, from the midst of a very hodge-podge of values, brings
out dimly a few traits, always wisely supported and walking,
so to speak, with crutches. But there is boldness about that
pencil line, sent out, with no landmarks to direct its course,
into the desert of the empty page. This line, which has to
find its own place and direction, and is not the uncertain
resultant of several trial marks, is as daring as an expedition
into the Sahara.
Lautrec put in his lines at arm's length, with astounding
swiftness and sureness of hand.
He had great facility, but he was not superficial. Whatever
he drew was what he meant to draw. It was something he had
seen and felt.

His masters, Bonnat and Cormon, had no difficulty in convincing him of the superiority of drawing over painting. He had been through sound advanced courses at school, and his intention was to express ideas. Now drawing is a more intellectual exercise than painting, which confines its appeal to the senses.

Nowhere in nature do I see a hard line drawn round the shapes of objects, sharply limiting the various values.

The border line between a field of lucerne grass and a field of wheat is indicated by the change from the green of the lucerne to the golden hue of the wheat. There is no artificial line, drawn between the two fields, from side to side, to answer to the pencil mark which shall divide off the surfaces of the fields in the drawing. The hard line is an invention of the mind, which needs some means of classification by which to see its way more clearly, and so draws up a well-defined, organised survey of the subject.

The colouring used by Lautrec is quite adequate for the expression of his thought. The old masters required no more.

The Impressionists, with their mania for light, brought in an Art with a sensual appeal, perhaps masking thought.

Lautrec, following the classical tradition, treated colour as an accompaniment. Yet his colouring, which does not aim at the illusion of light, is always an ornament of extreme distinction.

The bitterness of his view of things shews itself not only in his drawing, but also in his colouring. Lautrec frequently uses a certain lifeless, bitter shade of green. It is the tint of a kind of evening.

It is not the lovely blue-green of the twilight falling at the close of fine days, nor the blue of wet evenings, those moisture-laden twilights as brilliantly blue as stained glass. It is rather the sad green of dry, grey, neutral days.

Optimism is not his characteristic frame of mind.

The optimism of the Impressionists shews us cornfields

all golden beneath the morning sky, reapers, peasant women binding sheaves; a quiet farmstead wrapped in noon-day heat; the implements standing in the farmyard, and the beasts in the byre; fowl scooping out a nest in the dust, and crouching in it with their eyes closed; the siesta, the evening hour, and flower-scented gardens.

The Impressionist, charmed by the beauty of his subject, is eager to paint what he sees before him. But what he has before him may vary according as he glances a little to the right or the left. In his enthusiasm, he may act indiscriminately and select a bad point of view. Consequently his work will shew bad arrangement. But Lautrec, sitting quiet in his studio away from the world, has merely before him an untouched canvas, on which something beautiful is to be created. First of all, he surveys the rectangle, thinking out the arrangement of the picture. This explains why the setting out of his work is particularly careful.

I like Impressionist painting, and I am convinced that the great Impressionists were men of intellect. But, to be frank, their Art provides no certain proof of it. They say Sisley was a highly cultured man, of keen and even refined perceptions. His landscapes are exquisite. They throw me into the state of beatitude I experience when I view beautiful sights in nature. I cannot say they induce me to think a great deal. The painter seems to me a scarcely more intellectual agent than a photographic lens. On beholding his works you experience a sensation of delight. But are you inclined to voice your surprise, as when you hear a brilliant remark or a striking thought expressed? I think not.

Lautrec has much to impart. The interpretation of light is not his chief interest. He suggests many ideas. I believe I can make out a whole philosophy of life from his paintings. I understand what he loves. I arrive at that by elimination for what he detests he is at no pains to conceal.

◙

Lautrec made his début as a painter with several very bright canvases. *The Gunner Saddling his Horse* (1879, Albi Museum, No. 63) (Plate 1) is a work of striking effect and rich colouring. There is a feeling that the beginner took a delight in mixing up the pigments on his palette, compounding them, and trying the effect on the canvas. Whence came his faculty for such fine execution? Had Princeteau taught him all this, or was it a natural gift?

Perhaps, in the museum of his native town, young Lautrec had seen the large view of Venice by Guardi, an exquisite picture, which a painter could study for hours without tiring. On seeing this, very likely the boy made up his mind to use the same rich and intelligent colouring, with its fine texture, becoming weather-worn, flaky old stone to represent churches, and elsewhere fading and dissolving into the waters of the Grand Canal. Such a work may well determine a painter's vocation.

The *Gunner Saddling his Horse* is not exactly a good picture. The budding qualities it shews need maturing and building up. They put one in mind of this year's wine, a little sharp and thin. Nevertheless I do distinguish in this work that sheer joy in painting which I find in born painters, in Manet, for example, when he does still-lives or fruit. I cannot say as much of the products of those later years, when Lautrec fell a prey to a pervading sense of bitterness and gave his attention chiefly to expressive design.

The boy loved his work and made the most of every attractive sight that met his eye. In this same year, 1879, he painted *A Huntsman resaddling, At Gentilly races, A Horseman at Le Bosc;* some memories of the great manoeuvres at Le Bosc; *Mounted cuirassiers, Artillery in the field;* some American warships at Nice. In 1881, we have the *Portrait of Madame la Comtesse A. de Toulouse-Lautrec* at breakfast, at Malromé. This is a charming painting, daintily coloured and of very independent style. Then, in 1882, he did a number of views of Celeyran and *The Viaduct at Castel Vieil*, seen from the terrace of the family country-seat where he was born.

During 1882 he was painting nudes in Bonnat's studio. In the course of the summer vacation, he executed a score of charcoal portraits of relatives and friends. One of these, that of Count Charles de Toulouse-Lautrec, is in the Albi Museum (No. 71).

In 1883, in Cormon's studio, he painted a *Mythological subject : Icarus*, an *Allegory : The Springtime of life*, an *Elopement*, a *Prehistoric scene*, a *Primitive tribe*, and executed in charcoal a considerable number of carefully drawn studies from the nude. From that time forward he shewed himself more of a draughtsman than a painter. His colouring sobered down.

The year 1884 marks a return to « seen » subjects : *A Horseman Following the Hunt* and *A Cart sunk in the mud*.

In 1885 he painted some portraits : *Carmen, Suzanne Valadon*.

In 1886 we find him well in the swim of Montmartre nightlife : *At the Cabaret Bruant, At the Élysée-Montmartre*. He painted ballet-girls, too, as did Degas !

However, for several years past, nature had not been his only guide. He had been to exhibitions, and an influence became manifest in the arrangement of his subjects and in his choice of colours. *Young Ponty at Celeyran* (Albi Museum, No. 60) (Plate IV) and *A Labourer at Celeyran* (Albi Museum, No. 58) (Plate III), painted in 1882, are shewn sitting on grassy slopes. Their attitude, the green of the grass, and a certain shy suggestion of the open air, which we may consider as Impressionism toned down by the Beaux Arts, remind one of a painter who was at that time at the height of his glory : Bastien Lepage.

Then there is the influence of John Lewis Brown, the painter of horses, which has been pointed out by all Lautrec's biographers. It is noticeable in the *Mail Coach* (Nice, 1881) (Plate II) in the Musée de la Ville de Paris (Petit-Palais).

Up to this time Lautrec had shewn himself a very talented artist, but not yet very original. He had not yet discovered himself. He was swayed by a variety of influences. In the studios of Bonnat and Cormon draughtsmanship was urged before everthing else. But it was not long before Lautrec came to see that, though drawing may be excellent training for a painter, perfect designs make detestable groundwork for paintings. He saw that if the design itself is elaborated and carried to a finish, there is nothing more to add to the picture ; to colour it afterwards, that is to work in colour between fixed and unalterable lines, is an intolerable business for a painter ; furthermore, it is very difficult to avoid obliterating the drawing with the pigment, or to execute the colouring successfully, in view of the modelling, when the artist must all the time have an eye to the preservation of this precious design of his, which has already meant so much trouble.

◘

Then a fresh influence asserted itself, suggesting to Lautrec the means of overcoming this difficulty.

When he left Cormon's studio, he went to live with a friend of his named Grenier, at 19 bis, Rue Fontaine, in the very block of buildings where, down an alley-way, Degas had his studio. It is quite natural that people should have tried to shew the influence on Lautrec of this illustrious neighbour, who precisely at that time was abandoning prehistoric subjects. However, by coming back, as he did, to scenes of con-

temporary life, he was merely reverting to his early prefe-
rences, which had been counteracted by his training at Cormon's studio. A more decided influence is shewn in his imita-
tion of Degas' technique, but even then he keeps to his own
violent style and hatching. As a painter he never attained
that fine, clean craftsmanship, independent of all theory,
which Degas displayed in his great works : *Le foyer de la danse*
(1872), *Le pédicure* (1873), and *Les danseuses à la barre* (1877).
Such works, worthy of the Dutch masters, even of Vermeer,
reveal a love of nature and a pleasure in delicately handling
objects in light and atmosphere, which Lautrec, for years
past, had not sufficiently felt to take the risk of ruining his
design by attempting to spread fine colours over it.

◘

About the time Lautrec was making a beginning, Degas
was abandoning oils and taking up the drier medium of pastel.
At first he worked it over carefully, well covering the paper
(*The Green Singer*, 1884 ; *Dancers Bending*, 1885) ; but later,
from 1886 to the end, he used it with bold swift strokes, depic-
ting in this style women dressing, standing in the bath, or
drying themselves. By this means he was able to colour and
draw at the same time.

Pastel is a medium which allows the artist, while still making his design, to be already putting in his colour. He paints
and develops his drawing simultaneously, without any risk
of spoiling his lines : the ideal method !

So Lautrec went in for this bold stroke work too. He executed numerous paintings on cardboard by a procedure which
suited him admirably. He drew and shaded with brushes holding very thin colour. The cardboard absorbed the turpentine
and the oil, the colour remaining on the surface as smooth and
matt as pastel. This was drawing rather than painting.

The medium in question was employed in a number of compositions, among them the two pictures now in the Louvre *La Clownesse* (1895, Camondo Collection) and the *Portrait of M. Paul Leclercq* (1897).

These oil-paintings are often mistaken for pastel drawings, especially as they are small works. Larger sheets of cardboard would warp and pucker. They would have to be set on a rigid surface, involving an expense which the advantages of cardboard would not justify. Furthermore, with large surfaces, the hatching method becomes an endless business; spaces have to be covered by more rapid means. Then again, it is difficult to manage a large quantity of colour and work up modelling on cardboard, which sucks up the paint immediately. Accordingly, in his larger compositions (*Le Salon, La Danse du Boléro*), Lautrec painted on canvas. But he was very fond of working on cardboard, which, by taking the oil out of the colour, gave it a chalky appearance. On such a surface it was easy for him to bring out the deathly pale faces of tired revellers.

◻

When, after looking closely at some of Lautrec's pictures, you go into a restaurant or tea-rooms, or into any of those crowded places he was fond of frequenting, and watch the mixed crowd and the waitresses in their white aprons and black dresses striped by white shoulder-bands, you are quite surprised to find that there is a vigour and a power in the pictures which outdo reality itself. The impression made on the painter by such sights as these must have been particularly vivid, so powerfully are we struck by their reflection in his works. It is certain that he was no dilettante or frivolous observer, and he always worked with wholehearted sincerity. However, the technique he must have adopted, once he was clear of Cormon's studio, I mean that hatching method which freed him of the fear of ruining his design in process of colouring, contributed in no small degree to a characteristic clear-cut robustness which is scarcely ever attained in softly moulded work done entirely in oils.

Lautrec's compositions, with very little careful finish about them, but executed with clean precision, are not easily forgotten.

Hatching with colour does not lend itself to the expression of minute detail. The artist must have vision and work boldly for broad effect.

Even without this technique, it is not likely that Lautrec would have taken to the finical, precious type of work. As it was, it contributed greatly to the expression of his robust temperament.

Hatching is suitable for swiftly recorded inpressions which have to retain the nature of the sketch. It is also suitable for rough-sketching a picture which is later to be worked up carefully.

After all, how is the artist to set to work on a picture? With lines of colour, he can gradually modify the ground tint until little by little he reaches the exact tint required.

If, on the other hand, he uses the ordinary full-colour method, he as good as claims that he is able to put on the exact, final tint at once. It would take a very clever man indeed to mix this correctly, straightaway, without trial or modification. If the colour looks just right on the ground tint, it will appear quite otherwise when surrounded by other tints.

To proceed from one approximation to another is the logical way of working. The very first strokes, whether on primed canvas or cardboard, will bring out the exact tone, which cannot possibly be judged if the colour be daubed straight on to the clean surface.

Lautrec's thick strokes are done in fairly heavy tones. Even black is used. His is the forceful style of painting.

The soft bland effects of Impressionism would be ill-ren-

dered by this method. But Impressionism meant little to
Lautrec. What would be the use of delicate analyses of light
in pictures which owe their interest to vigorous, poster-like
contrasts?

Lautrec certainly did employ the division of tones, which
came from the Impressionists. He was induced to use it by
considerations of technique. He applied it literally, but not
in spirit. He applied it to the degree of monotony in the portrait of his mother reading (1885, Albi Museum, No. 53).
Again, in the picture *At the dressing table* (1898, Albi Museum,
No. 9), the properties, it is true, are caught by the evening
light and touched with bluish gleams. It is well done. Yet
when Vuillard paints tables laid in a café, at the same time
of the day, the whole melancholy of the evening twilight comes
over you as you gaze into the picture.

Striving after such an illusion is to-day rather despised.
This is largely because certain clever craftsmen, carrying
Impressionist theories too far, have realised light effects
which are simply astounding in their natural and undimmed
intensity. I remember seeing the blooms of some climbing
plant standing out brilliantly in the full glare of the sun
against the waters of the Mediterranean and the blue sky :
the eye could never encounter a more striking and unforget-
table sight. The effect was amazing. But this sort of thing
means one great sacrifice, that of the decorative point of
view.

There is a way of realising the illusion without sacrificing
the decorative qualities of painting : it must be possible to
regard the colours individually. No colour must be of so dis-
pleasing a tone as to repel the eye, as occasionally natural
colours do when they dazzle or produce halation.

With this reservation, I see no reason why truth in colour
should be in any way condemned.

Maurice Denis has written a theory to shew that striving

after the illusion of light is a base occupation, and that the old masters never troubled about it. Yet he himself has succeeded in rendering luminous effects with perfect charm. The truth is he is too healthy a spirit to keep his pleasure to himself. He feels light is too beautiful !

By contrast, Lautrec's subjects are sombre and bitter.

The portraits he did by the hatching method in the garden of his old neighbour Forest, at the bottom of the Rue Caulin-court, were not painted in the open air (1889 : *A Woman's Head, A Red-Haired Woman, Woman with a Sunshade;* 1890 : *Gabrielle la Danseuse, Deaf Bertha;* 1891 : *Gabrielle la Danseuse, Justine Dieuhl, Mlle Honorine P.*).

He reverted to the garish technique of his earlier days in several simple figures : *Stout Maria* (1884), *Carmen* (1885), *Red-Faced Rosa* (1888), *The Washerwoman* (1889), exercises in portraiture which did not require intricate planning and drawing.

Were it not for this series of works I should wonder why Lautrec, who, like Degas, nearly always worked with lines of colour, did not go off into pastel, as the more illustrious artist did.

The fact is he never gave up the idea of reverting on occasion to modelling in full colour. In his heart of hearts he remained attached to oils.

He gave up pure painting on choosing his career as an artist in satirical drawing, for which he felt he was suited, but he always felt a longing to go back to it.

These portraits, full of purely plastic qualities, were for him relaxations from the task he had set himself, unconsciously perhaps, of doing more intellectual work.

One fine day even the painter with most theories in his head will throw the whole lot overboard and enjoy himself painting with the greatest simplicity : a simplicity which is more apparent than real, for the knowledge acquired is still there and gives warning against the pitfalls that lie all along the way. Corot as a painter of figures had this kind of simplicity, so had Bonvin, Bazille, Guillaume Régamey, and many other good artists who, in the nineteenth century, did not enjoy the reputation they deserved.

◉

Lautrec lived for a time with his friend Grenier, then with Doctor Bourges at 21 Rue Fontaine. In 1893, the Doctor married, so he moved into the Rue Ganneron and lived with Rachon, a painter from Toulouse. Later he obtained funds from his parents and made a home for himself, first at 7 Rue Tourlaque, then at 27, Rue Caulincourt, and finally, 1897, at 5 Avenue Frochot. He never moved far from the Moulin-Rouge.

His mother lived only a short distance away. He used to go and have meals with her. When he was unwell she came and nursed him. When at last he died, she gathered up the pictures he left and presented them to the city of Albi, where they went to form the Lautrec Museum in the Palais de la Berbie. He left a great many works, for he scarcely ever sold any. His finest portraits were those of relatives and friends. No fine-art fancier ever ordered anything from him. La Goulue refused to sit for him and Lavallière was very annoyed by a portrait he did of her. She considered it a horrid joke!

◉

By entering thus the Palais de la Berbie, Henri de Toulouse-Lautrec, whose ancestors had reigned by fortune of arms over Languedoc and Albigeois and lost these provinces in the hazards of war, entered one of the finest palaces of their former states, there to reign in peace by the prestige of his genius alone.

La Berbie was formerly the palace of the Archbishops of Albi, which city, writes Moreri, « was raised to the Archbishopric in the year 1678 by Innocent XI at the instance of Louis XIV ».

The building of this palace had been decided upon in 1265 by Bishop Bernard de Combret. His successor Bernard de Castanet went on with it and furthermore undertook, in 1282, the construction of the cathedral of Saint Cecilia. These two fine brick structures form an imposing and charming *ensemble*.

The bishops of Albi, one after another, enlarged and embellished the mansion. About the middle of the xvii[th] century Gaspard de Daillon du Lude had the monumental staircase put in leading to the museum.

Next door to Cardinal de Bernis' collection, which contains the beautiful large view of Venice by Guardi, there is a gallery, formerly used as the archbishops' library, in which you will find Lautrec's posters and lithographs. His drawings, the portraits his friends did of him, his palette and the lithographic stone *Portrait of Bruant* are preserved in a circular hall through which you have to pass to reach the great picture gallery.

If you are to understand Lautrec, you must see this museum. Nowhere else will you find such a collection of his paintings. You will see that the quality of several of the works on exhibition is remarkable.

Moreover the place itself is delightful. From the balconies which skirt the galleries there is a fine view of the city and the surrounding country.

■

In 1891, Lautrec often went to the hospital with his cousin Doctor Tapié de Celeyran, and these visits gave the painter ideas for several sketches and two pictures : *An operation on the trachea performed by Doctor Péan at the International Hospital* (Plate VI) and *An operation by Doctor Péan at the International Hospital.*

As indicated by their titles, these two pictures depict surgical operations. Yet, in the second, there is no patient visible, and all we see of the doctor is his back. The resident students are grouped about their chief in the great operating theatre. The interest of this work lies in the composition.

The other picture, *An operation on the trachea,* is a portrait of Doctor Péan. There is violence in this portrait, as there is in the surgical operation. Streaks of colour on a ground of unprimed cardboard indicate the lights of the face : they follow the ridges of the muscles contracted by strain and physical effort.

It is a magnificent and terrible portrait.

Doctor Tapié de Celeyran had come to Paris to study medicine. As he wandered wearily round the bars and music-halls, it was visible that he was pining for the old life in the country.

After Lautrec's death he went back to live in his native district and never moved from it again.

Lautrec was sincerely fond of him. He loved, the queer contrast of their figures. In *A Table at the Moulin-Rouge* (1892) (Plate VIII) we see them walking side by side, the painter scurrying along and the Doctor taking tremendous strides.

Lautrec was something of a bully to this bland companion of his. He made his poor cousin bear all the brunt of his bad moods, for he was quick-tempered and could brook no opposition to his whims.

When the light failed and it was no longer possible to distinguish the colours on the palette, the two cousins used to take a stroll as far as the Bar Achille, at 4 Rue Scribe. After exchanging his soft studio hat for a bowler, which he wore well tilted over his forehead, Lautrec would start out to walk there. He got along with great difficulty. He used to stop and rest on his stick, and, as though to justify the pause, usually gave out some opinion in a guttural voice, with his head bent, as though sunk in deep meditation. At this pace the journey from Montmartre to the Bar Achille used to be a long one.

This bar, which rejoiced in the name of « The Cosmopolitan », was the meeting place of artists and writers who were not connected with the Beaux-Arts or the French Academy. Mallarmé frequented it.

In this little circle, when a writer announced that he was going to publish a book, Lautrec would design a cover for it, and even draw the illustrations. His friends knew he had a good heart and loved him for it.

However, in his own way, he was quite a character. If he saw a fresh customer come into the bar, whose looks he did not care for, he would tip the « patron » the wink to disregard the intruder, so that he should be in no hurry to come again. Big Achille, knowing that the success of his bar depended very largely on Lautrec's presence, whose brilliant rejoinders and sweeping wit attracted many to the place, willingly submitted to this tyranny, which after all had no real harm in it.

Lautrec's ideas shewed constant development. In the so-called pleasure-haunts he was always at work. He was amassing stores of information, from which he built with steady, unremitting effort a lasting monument of art. I wonder if we understand what such a life-sentence of forced labour must mean? When others are indulging in recreation, the painter is hard at work. Do we understand the effort of memory required to keep in the mind and classify such a number of traits observed? *A Table at the Moulin-Rouge* contains portraits of Monsieur Édouard Dujardin, la Macarona, Paul Sescau, Maurice Guibert, Mademoiselle Nelly C..., Doctor Tapié de Celeyran and the artist himself. It is a complete set of characters expressed and values recorded. Then, apart from the subject itself, with its finely realised main masses, there is a whole host of details : the back of a chair, the end of a table, the mirror-frames, the globes of the lights, hats of various shapes and all kinds of furs. These things seem unimportant yet they all have to be carefully studied and represented, for they lend reality to the scene. In a prehistoric scene, however deeply the painter may have studied his subject, details of this kind are all too obviously fictitious.

A Table at the Moulin-Rouge is a whole world in itself. Lautrec could not paint such a picture on the spot. He had to build up the work in his mind; he had actually to create it.

When an artist has been struck by some characteristic scene, the emotion he has experienced sets going the machinery of his imagination. As the mind dwells on it, the impression grows and becomes exaggerated, so much so that the sight of the real thing would come as a damper.

As Puvis de Chavannes was travelling by train through the lowlands of the Somme, he noticed a lovely landscape, redolent of the sense of nobility and calm. He kept it in mind for the attendant scene of his first Saint-Genevieve of the Pantheon. When he mentioned it to his friends, some-one asked him if he were going back to the spot to work direct from nature. « No », he answered, « I should be afraid of dulling my first impression ». It is necessary, of course, when this first impression is established in sketch form, to view a second time the details of the subject, to avoid getting anything too glaringly incorrect or too far removed from reality. To use the expression of Delacroix, the artist has to look up his words in the dictionary of nature.

However, I can quite understand Puvis de Chavannes' fear of losing his grip on the subjects as seen in the imagination, and I see the point of view of the peasant who, when asked what he thought of Paris, replied : « I could not see the city for the houses. »

Yet one has to admit that painting done direct from nature has a sincerity of tone which work done in the studio cannot capture. The fact is the painter gets disheartened by the fatigue occasioned before the sitting by the transport of all his weighty apparatus, the colour box, the easel and the canvas. All this worry and encumbrance takes the edge off his appreciation of the beauty of nature.

There is another view to take of this question. If, with the aid of a rough drawing made on a leaf of a small sketchbook, he can revive the memory of all the elements of a landscape or any other kind of scene, how free and unencumbered he will feel as he wanders in search of a subject! Why, everything he sees will seem worthy of interpretation! He will see beauty in every view!

Along he goes, taking down rapid notes : seeds that shall germinate in the hot-house of the studio. How easy it is! The painter has but to look about him : the whole world is his!

Having observed subjects for pictures at the Moulin-Rouge, Lautrec recorded these and painted his pictures with concentrated and unflagging effort. Can we wonder that he was self-willed in everyday matters?

Toward his parents he was respectful but firm. When his father, worried and disappointed over him, used to say : « I wish he would keep to accepted masters! If only he would study Detaille! » he paid no heed. A good thing too!

Opportunist, manoeuvring characters, may pass through the midst of the human crowd and through events without taking any grip on them or bearing them along. They dodge between. They may do something in politics, which may be defined as a game of holding the balance. But such minds cannot realise or create anything new. To be a leader and master of events, a man has to be stern, and first of all to himself. Lautrec worked hard. The annoyance caused him by other people's stupidity induced him to be somewhat impertinent. But he was merely saying in his own way : « Let me get on with my work. »

He was sometimes the victim of very cruel rejoinders. One night, at Maxim's, he had been very brilliant, too much so for the liking of the people sitting near, who were the victims of his witty discourse and the subjects of his sketches. He got up to go, leaving on his table a pencil worn to a little stump. When seated he looked quite presentable, for the upper part of his body was of normal build. But his poor legs ! When he stood on them he was shorter than when he was seated on a chair. Just as he was going, one of his neighbours called him back and held out the pencil, saying : « Here you are, sir, you have forgotten your walking-stick ! »

He had the grace not to complain, but even to laugh, on occasion, at his physical oddity. One evening, at the Moulin-Rouge, two women seated at a small table were having an argument. One was boasting of her dog's pedigree. The other made a grimace and said she thought it was an ugly creature. The owner rejoined : « Look here, the roof of his mouth is quite black. That is a sure sign of a thoroughbred. » Then, turning suddenly to a gentleman who was sitting behind her at the next table — it was Lautrec — she invited him to bear out her statement : « It is possible, isn't it, to be very ugly and yet be a thoroughbred? » — « Perhaps that is meant for me ! » was his reply, bringing his hand to his forehead in a military salute, palm to the front : a palm that was black with charcoal !

His breed ! He was very proud of his ancestors, proud of their crimes as well as their exploits.

In 1214, one of them, Raimond VI, Comte de Toulouse, had his own brother Baudouin hanged. As though Heaven meted out punishment on earth for this terrible act, his son Raimond VII died childless and thereafter the Counts of Toulouse descended from the murdered brother.

An unshakeable will, joined with a complete contempt for the opinion of the ignorant, is apt to bring on the habit of running counter to opinion of this sort on every possible occasion.

For example, those who visit exhibitions do not understand that the interest of a work of art lies in the arrangement of the values far more than in the subject. In his picture *L'Absinthe* Degas has painted the portrait of Marcellin Desboutin. The figure, in his scheme of values, is logically placed right against the frame. The model is relegated to a corner. The Japanese, who were then just beginning to be appreciated, gave a lead in arrangements of this kind. Lautrec too, in *A Table at the Moulin-Rouge*, placed a gigantic, strange figure right away from the centre of the canvas. By reason of its expression, but not its value, this will draw the eyes of the uninitiated, when actually the real subject of the picture is to be found well to the middle.

Nevertheless, one critic did Lautrec a good turn in this connection. In the course of a study devoted to our artist's work (In the « Figaro illustré », April 1902), Monsieur Arsène Alexandre, entirely on his own responsibility, reproduced this same picture with broad strips cut away from the bottom and the right-hand side. In this way the large figure and the uninteresting balustrade which cuts across were brought into the foreground. The reproduction was thereby much improved. The figures of Lautrec and his cousin the Doctor, which claim our special interest, gain in importance. The pictorial subject and the intrinsic idea now coincide. Their original incongruity was perplexing to present-day specta tors, who cannot appreciate that such a work was done, like Degas' *Absinthe*, in the spirit of a challenge. The fight has long been over, and this remains as a sort of wager that looks to us as though it were conceived with the rather puerile object of astonishing the Philistines.

It is true that Lautrec often surprised the gallery unintentionally. He would sleep in his studio in the daytime, as is

shewn by a photograph published by Gustave Coquiot.
There was nothing extraordinary in that. When a man has
spent the night observing and working from his model,
whether at the Moulin-Rouge or elsewhere, he needs rest.
Lautrec saw to it that no opportunity was missed of making
up for lost sleep. Whenever he had to travel by train, he was
no sooner settled in his compartment than he dropped off
to sleep. When he was at London on one occasion, exhibiting
a collection of his works, he went to sleep on a seat as he was
waiting for the Prince of Wales to come and view his pictures.
He was so fast asleep that the Prince specially requested that
he should not be awakened. He also used to sleep in the cab
which took him home at night, and if the driver tried to rouse
him, he strongly objected to getting out, and went on snoring
until he felt like going in to bed. Finally he would repair to
his room, carrying under his arm some bread, dinner-sausage
and a bottle of wine. We cannot but wonder at the fine tem-
per of his constitution, which speedily recuperated every
time after crushing exertions. One thing eventually overcame
this resistance, and that was the abuse of alcohol.

How did a cripple, who lived an irregular life, manage
to put out such an enormous quantity of work? The fact is
his digestion was excellent and his constitution, apart from
acquired complaints and alcoholic poisoning, generally speaking sound. It is my idea that he owed his good health to
those childhood years spent at Albi. The bracing air you
breathe away on those uplands which slope down steeply to
the Tarn, is a sharpener for the appetite. There you drink a
lightish, mellow country-gentleman's wine which stimulates
the digestion and fills the mind with warm, rosy ideas, as
rosy-tinted, shall we say, as the cathedral, the Palais de la
Berbie and the old mansions of the Albigeois gentry. The
house Lautrec lived in had been given to his family by the
Du Bosc ladies, who owned the Château du Bosc. Hence the

name of Hôtel du Bosc, sometimes given to the mansion in which the Toulouse-Lautrec and Tapié de Celeyran families lived together. From the terrace of the house you see the viaduct of Castel-Vieil, which Lautrec painted in 1881, looming up beyond a broad drive and great lawns.

◘

At the Moulin-Rouge Lautrec found varied and strongly characterised models. The one he gave most attention to was obviously la Goulue. She is the subject of the poster he did in 1891 for the establishment, also of *A Rest between two Waltzes* (1891) (Plate VII). She is a fine young woman.

In 1892, he drew her again in *La Goulue entering the Moulin-Rouge* (Plate IX). We see her coming straight towards us, arm in arm with her sister and a woman friend. She alone is dressed and hatless. It is evident from her bold and confident bearing that she is quite at home in the place. « Incessu patuit dea ». She is entering her palace, attended by her ladies-in-waiting. She is a queen, but a queen in search of courtiers. The sidelong glance and mobile lips lure the men as she passes by. Her face is seductive and tormented. Her corsage is all disarranged, and the dip of the gaping bodice ill conceals the flattish, drooping breasts. All this means debauch, and low debauch at that. Lautrec shews himself a moralist here.

It is extremely difficult for a sculptor or a painter to express the seductiveness of a face, when its charm, very different from classical beauty, comes from a certain mobility of the features, from the shifting gleam of the eyes, in a word from all that reveals the moral being.

I appreciate without effort the charm of the Greek profile on exhibition at the Louvre under the title (which I believe to be inexact) of « Medusa's Head », in that fine room which contains the « Venus Raising her Draping », so much admired

3

by Degas. That disturbing yet classical profile thrills me to the very fibres of my being. I feel that some inherited strain, coming down through two thousand years, fated me to love her.

And yet, in this same Museum, when I have stood looking at the portrait of the beautiful Madame Récamier, or that of Madame Chalgrin, so madly beloved of David that he had her guillotined, or that of the Comtesse Regnault de St. Jean d'Angely by Gérard, I have often wondered what made for the reputation of these celebrated women. The intrinsic nature of their charm was very likely divined with greater delicacy and perception by their portraitists than by anyone else, yet even these have not been able to utter it.

I am at a loss to understand how Lautrec could have fallen so much under charm of the English girl at the Star at Havre as to break his journey to paint her.

In July 1899 he intended travelling to Taussat, and, as was his custom, instead of going by train to Bordeaux and Arcachon, he was going to board a ship at Havre. But there he met the English girl, and there his journey ended. The seductive charm of this woman, with her lively, pert sort of face and tilted nose, was doubtless due to smiling eyes, a clear, pretty voice and a very animated manner which is not amenable to representation in plastic art. Her portrait (Albi Museum, No. 47) (Plate XIX) is a delightful piece of work. Yet I feel that the admiration it arouses in people who view it is nothing like the exalted feeling the artist experienced at the time and wished to communicate.

On the other hand, it is with terrible effectiveness that Lautrec reveals to us the vicious allurements of La Goulue's face as she walks down the hall of the Moulin-Rouge.

I hope she will not be angry with me if she happens to read these lines. I hope Paul Leclercq the novelist will not bear me any grudge either. We are not really concerned with

la Goulue herself, or with Paul Leclercq, but with the works
of the artist's imagination. We are considering Lautrec, not
as the painter of their portraits, but as an artist at work in
their presence, taking them, if you like, as pretexts for pictures. He practised « free use of the model », and in the separate interpretations of a single model we sometimes find
such differences that the person concerned is unrecognisable.
Who can honestly say he recognises La Goulue of 1892 in the
engraving of 1895, in which she appears as a circus-trainer?
The graces of youth which Lautrec had denied the noisy
vampire of the Moulin-Rouge he dispensed liberally three
years later to the circus-trainer. Here she appears as a fine,
lithe figure, long in the leg, arched and supple. It is a drawing
which might well be signed « March ».

La Goulue, it is true, grew stouter as the years went by.
But did she grow taller? In the *Rest between two Waltzes*
(1891) (Plate VII), her height is seven and three-quarter heads,
and in the engraving of 1895 eight and a quarter. This seems
to imply that, in four years, she grew taller by half a head!
What, at her age? Of course not. Lautrec was simply flatte-
ring her.

There is further proof that he harboured no grudge against
her, for in 1895 he did her a service by painting two panels,
each three metres square, intended for a fair-booth.

Then again, in the picture of 1892, *A Table at the Moulin-
Rouge*, La Goulue is seen in the back-ground rearranging her
hair before a mirror with a charming gesture, full of style.

In his desire to bring out the essential lines of a figure,
Lautrec habitually exaggerated some trait which struck
him as particularly characteristic. He would draw out a figure
to slimmer proportions, make it taller or perhaps more squat.
He altered a person's build for a purpose. Now the figure of
La Goulue's usual dancing partner, Boneless Valentin, was
so striking that Lautrec had no need to exaggerate. All he

had to do in this case was to copy from life. The various representations he has given us of this model are all stamped with a strong resemblance and shew remarkable development in the artist's ideas.

This Valentin, whose expressionless, English-looking face seemed as though it were hewn out of a sphere of oak, was the brother of a Parisian lawyer. He was usually seen riding before lunch in the Bois de Boulogne. In the afternoon he travelled round making calls for his brother. In the evening he danced at the Moulin de la Galette and the Moulin-Rouge with La Goulue, Grille d'Egout and Nini-Patte-en-l'Air. He danced for the love of the art. He was never paid for his performances. His agility and the swift precision of his whirling legs were inimitable. His queer figure gave endless amusement to the crowd. One can quite understand that he made an ideal model for Lautrec's pencil.

In the Moulin-Rouge poster (1891) (Plate xxv), we see la Goulue dancing in the full glare of the lights with her leg raised rather high, and then, standing in the foreground to set off the effect, we descry Valentin, with his hand to his mouth, in so eloquent an attitude that we can almost hear him saying : Shocking !

He is the principal figure on the left-hand panel of the circus-girl's booth (1895). He is dancing with la Goulue. The scene had been done before. The panel is merelly an enlargement of sketch No. 57 in the Albi Museum entitled *Boneless Valentin and la Goulue at the Moulin de la Galette* (1888). Valentin's legs are the real subject of the picture. They are wide apart and rigidly braced in a most grotesque position.

They are also the subject of the picture *The dance at the Moulin-Rouge* (1890). Here they twist and twirl with incredible suppleness. La Goulue is dancing. People are on the move all round. The picture is crammed with life, noisy, deafening. On the floor, the light, set a-whirl by la Goulue and Valentin, joins in the dance.

The « free use of the model » induced Lautrec, in his poster for the *Artisan moderne* (1894), to represent the medal-engraver Henri Nocq as a craftsman of tall, slim build.

In the two portraits he executed from the same model (1897) (Plate XVII), he worked for caricature, altering the feet and legs for some premeditated reason. Monsieur Nocq, on shewing me these portraits, of which he is justly proud, said with a smile : « He was merciless with me ! »

The portrait he did of the Doctor in a theatre corridor is equally unkind.

Occasionally the two cousins went in the orchestra stalls at the Comédie Française. After nights spent at the Moulin-Rouge, Lautrec appreciated by contrast the respectability of the theatre. He was not greatly taken up with outstanding productions and star actresses. What he loved to watch was a repertoire piece with some second-rate actor on fixed pay, without a future, the understudy hack who, puffed out with pride, rolled his r's, slashed out great gestures and made awful eyes !

So much for the satirical view. Now and again, however, he yielded to the charm of beauty and talent, as proved by his lithographs, in which you will find lines caressed with loving skill.

He has portrayed the Doctor in a dim, quiet theatre corridor. Through the open door of a box we catch a glimpse of the ruddy, brilliantly lit auditorium. The curious figure, the semi-darkness through which it is seen dimly moving, the glimpse of the open theatre, make a very fine picture, a complete work and a true Lautrec, full of malicious implication.

Lautrec did not consider it wise to make so free with all his models. The portrait of his cousin Louis Pascal (1893, Albi Museum, No. 35) (Plate X) and that of Monsieur Fourcade

(1889) shew gentlemen of immaculate and fashionable appearance. The style, too, of these pictures is very elegant and attractive, making them fit for the walls of the richest drawing-room. We detect Lautrec's hand, however, in the animation of the figures. Monsieur Fourcade is walking. Monsieur Louis Pascal has just stopped. Nevertheless he is still intensely alive.

Jane Avril, to take another case, is never still. Lautrec portrays her as slender, wiry, for ever a-whirl, well-deserving of her familiar name Mélinite. While La Goulue, between two waltzes, takes a stroll round with her partner (1891), Jane Avril, in the middle view, is seen executing pirouettes.

Lautrec did many paintings and drawings of her.

In 1892 he produced the following studies : *Jane Avril leaving the Moulin-Rouge — Dancing — Putting on her Gloves — In a fur Cape and Hat with Feathers — In Profile — In the Japanese Divan* (preliminary study for the poster figuring Yvette Guilbert and Édouard Dujardin).

In 1893 : *Jane Avril Dancing* (study for the Jardin de Paris poster) — *Bust with hat — Bust without hat — In Profile* (study for the cover of the original engraving).

Working with la Goulue as his model, Lautrec's intention was to depict sensual charm. With Jane Avril he sought the expression of movement.

The serpentine, luminous dancing of Loïe Fuller at the Folies-Bergère was the subject of one painting (Albi Museum, No. 32) and one lithograph (Delteil 39).

For him, Yvette Guilbert symbolised the subtlest of spirits, entirely freed from the fetters of matter.

Unlike La Goulue, who had previously refused to come to the crippled artist's studio to pose for him, Yvette Guilbert, on being asked, was only to pleased to comply. She was celebrated and had a great welcome wherever she went. But a singer's success does not last for ever. So at the artist's call glory came. And he acquitted himself right royally toward the obliging lady, for it is by the paintings and the two albums of lithographs he devoted to her that she will live in the memory of men who never heard her sing.

These paintings, executed in 1894, are as follows :

Yvette Guilbert's Black Gloves (study for the cover of the French Album).

Yvette Guilbert (sketch for a poster, Albi Museum, No. 146).

Yvette Guilbert Taking a Call (study for the sixteenth lithograph in the album, Albi Museum, No. 112) (Plate XXXIII).

Yvette Guilbert, Linger Longer Loo (preliminary sketch for the drawing for « Le Rire », December 24, 1894).

□

Eight years after leaving the official studios, Lautrec had produced a large number of pictures, yet his reputation was still limited to a small circle of close friends. It was by his lithographs that he eventually became known, and it was through this medium that his faculties found their most complete expression.

The first time he used the lithographic pencil, he very likely said to himself : « This is the very thing for me ! » I say the lithographic pencil, not ink. For his first lithograph *At Saint-Lazare* (1885) could not give him an adequate idea of his gifts in this direction. It is a plain drawing in ink, without any kind of modelling. So he was in no hurry to make another attempt. However, in 1891, Zidler gave him an order for a poster for the Moulin-Rouge. This time he produced a masterpiece : *La Goulue* (Plate XXV). It is a most cunningly designed placard, composed of large light and dark shapes, finely arranged to arrest the attention of passers-by, and describing a very beautiful arabesque.

Lautrec was greatly encouraged by the complete success of

this poster. On witnessing the transfer process, he felt he would like to work on the stone himself. So he executed two coloured lithographs : *La Goulue and her Sister at the Moulin-Rouge* and *The Englishman at the Moulin-Rouge* (1892), which, by reason of their large shapes of plain colour, are really posters on a small scale.

It was also in 1892 that he painted *La Goulue entering the Moulin-Rouge* (Plate IX).

For eight years he had been treating all his subjects by the hatching method ; only the year before (1891), he had produced *A Rest between two Waltzes* (Plate VII). But now this artist, who had undergone the influence first of Guardi, then of John Lewis Brown, Bastien Lepage and Degas, having once executed a successful poster, fell, so to speak, under his own influence. The art of lithography proved irresistibly attractive to him, and, in the picture painted in 1892, we find him using large coloured shapes as in lithograph.

He was further urged to this new method by a desire to realise a more complete representation of the model's face. Using lines of colour, it is only possible to produce summary effects. To work up delicate modelling, the strokes have to be drawn very close to one another and even run together. This was Lautrec's procedure in the celebrated portrait of La Goulue in *A Table at the Moulin-Rouge* (1892) (Plate VIII), *The Doctor in a Theatre Corridor* (1894) and the *Portrait of Madame Pascal at the Piano* (1895) (Plate XIV).

Yet he seemed unable to make up his mind, for at the very time he was painting these pictures with close, welded hatching, we find him painting others with clearly separated strokes : *A Couple Dancing, the Start of the Quadrille, Jane Avril* (1892) ; *Portrait of M. Louis Pascal* (1893) (Plate X) ; *In Bed* (1894) ; *The Washerman* (Plate XII) ; *Monsieur et Madame* (Plate XIII) ; *La Clownesse* (1895).

He never definitely decided for either method.

In 1892 he did more posters : *Hanged* (for the « Dépêche de

Toulouse ») ; *The Japanese Divan* (another masterpiece) ;
Queen of Joy (to advertise a novel by Victor Joze) ; *Bruant*
(for the Ambassadeurs) ; *Bruant* (for the Eldorado).

◻

Colour-engraving has a very definite influence on a painter's craft, because it presents difficulties of quite a new
order. When designing wood-cuts or lithographs, the artist
has to set apart rectangles and other clean-cut shapes for
printing in such and such a colour. He has to be very careful
not to go over his line and get colour on a surface that is set
apart. For the engraver, putting in a coloured shape does not
mean spreading colour over a certain part of the ground. He
has first to survey carefully his block or plate, then outline
the shape, and finally colour it in with the strictest attention
to its exact tone, value and degree of purity. It is not until
the block is printed that the artist will see if he has made a
mistake. How easy and convenient are ordinary oils in com-
parison ! If the pigment has been daubed on at random, it
may be scraped off with the palette knife, or it may be painted over without being removed at all. Any mistake can be
retrieved. This technique encourages a certain carelessness,
which passes into the painter's art and becomes a trait of his
character.

The craft of engraving is a more stringent business. Not
only does it modify the painter's manner, but the constant
preoccupation of setting apart surfaces on his plates for the
individual expression of each value and tone, makes the artist
look for tones and values in nature as subjects for exact interpretation. He begins to look upon them as all-important !
They impart to the humblest sight a deep interest, and the
artist comes to regard nature with other eyes than those of
the mere painter.

No easy, haphazard daubing will do in this branch of art.

The picture has to be planned and studied beforehand. The care and effort exacted lend greater earnestness to the artist's work. The finished picture has more idea of construction about it.

Furthermore, the painter comes to see that he has to eliminate or simplify many things in his subject, which, if rendered in detail, would involve him in endless and tiresome complications. This touches one of the fundamentals of artistic expression.

But colour-engraving is not properly speaking lithography, the art in which Lautrec was to display his full powers.

The cover he executed in 1893 for « L'Estampe originale », representing Jane Avril standing beside the printer and his press, examining a proof, is really a small coloured poster.

It was only by working with the pencil on the stone itself, that he finally realised the sensitive design and delicate modelling which we find in the celebrated portrait of « Bruant » (1893) and in the twelve pictures drawn for the paper L'Escarmouche (1893-1894) (Plates XXVI, XXVII, XXVIII, XXIX).

In the portrait of « Bruant », besides pencil lines, we still see brush marks and crachis. Later on, the clean line prevailed and ink surfaces entirely disappeared.

A black and white lithograph is after all merely a design executed on stone, a straightforward method of work, enabling the artist to devote himself entirely to expression, without being harassed by technique.

When a horse-dealer wishes to train a horse to step high, he puts very heavy shoes on him. The horse has to make a great effort to lift his hoofs. When this effort has become a habit with him, the heavy shoes are taken off and he then easily raises his knees nose-high.

A painter who has sustained without faltering the heavy technique of colour-engraving, will find black and white lithography quite easy, and, having become accustomed to hard, searching toil, will express still better through a simple medium ideas which he has already successfully interpreted through a complicated one.

Lautrec drew direct on the stone.

However, it has become the practise to execute designs with the lithographic pencil on a special kind of paper, and then have them transferred to the stone.

This method has several advantages. The artist can take the paper with him in his portfolio and work straight from the subject, whereas the stone cannot be taken from the studio. Moreover, as the transfer of the design to the stone reverses it once, the print comes off the right way round.

On the other hand, what troubles of a purely artistic order may arise! If perchance the grain of the paper does not coincide exactly with that of the stone, the lines may be over-stressed in places and faint and broken in others. When the transfer has not taken in certain parts, and the artist has to retouch the stone to patch up his design, the retouched lines, being regular, look clean and light beside the shaky lines which necessarily result from the haphazard contact of the two different grains.

In the art of pure monochrome lithography Lautrec straightway touched perfection, and in the course of the next eight years produced an astonishing series of master-pieces. As early as 1893, we have a composition entitled *Folies-Bergère : Les pudeurs de M. Prud'homme* (Plate XXVII), in which Lautrec displays astounding skill in the manipulation of blacks, greys and whites.

From 1894 to 1896 he produced those perfect works, the stage portraits : *Lenoir, Moreno* (Plate XXX) ; *Yvette Guilbert* (Plates XXXI, XXXII, XXXIII) ; *Marcelle Lender* (Plate XXXIV) ; *Auguez* (Plate XXXV) ; *Jeanne Granier, Guitry, Miss Ida Heath* (Plate XXXVI), and finally that beautiful series of female studies *Elles* (Plate XXXVIII).

What craftsmanship! What freedom!

Now he draws with the point of the pencil, now he works with it flat, covering broad surfaces as though with a wide brush : *Princely Idyll* (1897) ; *At the Théâtre Libre : Antoine in Trouble* (January, 1894). No-one has used with greater success the artifice of bringing out some happy trait in dead black from surrounding soft greys, almost from white : for example the black bow of the periwig in *Fortunio's Song* (Plate xxxv) ; the black cat in *Miss May Belfort taking a Call* (1895) ; *Yvette Guilbert's Black Gloves* (Plate xxxi) ; Miss Ida Heath's bodice (1896) (Plate xxxvi).

And what extraordinary variety of expression! Those faces of Yvette Guilbert's in the sixteen lithographs devoted to her in the French Album! (Plates xxxi, xxxii, xxxiii). Those gestures of hers, those attitudes, now astonished, now roguish, always amazingly clever! How delicately Lautrec has rendered all these shades of expression by means of a touch of black on a light ground!

Rose Caron in Faust (1894) (Plate xxviii), on the other hand is a frightful caricature. Her singing partner has his mouth open wide enough to unhinge his jaw! Rose Caron contracts the muscles of her face... to emit a note?... or is she going to sneeze? One cannot help laughing at this drawing.

The most striking thing about all these works is their animation.

Movement! Lautrec regretted to the last his inability to join in sport. He was often at the Vélodrome Buffalo, of which his friend Tristand Bernard was manager. He used to walk about among the athletes, admiring their muscles and jotting down notes. In 1893 he drew Tristan Bernard exercising his functions as starter. In the same year he produced three lithographs on sporting subjects : *Zimmermann and his Machine, At the Velodrome : W. D. Simpson and Little Michael* and *At the Velodrome*. In 1896 he executed two posters : *The Mickael cycle* and *The Simpson Chain*.

He caught his models in full action. It was their movement that enthused and inspired him. Getting people to pose
and arranging their attitude was not his method. A friend of
his whose portrait he was anxious to paint, as a gracious and
friendly compliment, confesses that the sittings were rather
irksome. Lautrec would send for him, sit him down, put in a
few touches with the brush, then say : « It is too fine to stay
in. Let us go for a stroll ! » This comedy was repeated a score
of times. And yet he only had to catch a glimpse of a quick,
nimble dancer (La Mélinite) or the mobile face of an actress
(Yvette Guilbert or Marcelle Lender) and the play of limb or
feature was recorded in an instant.

Fortunio's Song (Plate XXXV) is perhaps the culminating
point of Lautrec's Art. Too often his Art was marred by
bitterness. In the long run recriminations weary us. But in
this work there is no disparaging suggestion whatsoever. It is
sheer beauty. The lines of these two people singing side by
side are worthy of Watteau. The whole idea is purity itself.
As to values : Marcelle Lender merges into the greys of the
background ; Marguerite Auguez in the foreground, dressed
as a man, is white with light from head to foot, with a black
bow at her periwig. These three colours, grey, white and black,
distributed with perfect tact, play a delightful harmony.

If he had often had models such as these, instead of the
music-hall women he had to manage with, who knows what
he would have done?

But no woman of fashion ever thought of going to him to
have her charms preserved for posterity. He was able to
sketch figures at the theatre because the actresses could not
conceal themselves. Several consented to pose specially for
him, and they had no cause to regret it.

◻

Among these delightful compositions and such deeply

intelligent portraits, I discover to my dismay some slack, ill-formed designs which nevertheless have been honoured by reproduction. They are certainly not without their humour. If a child had scrawled them, you would say he was clever and comical. But I must say, at first sight the absence of plastic qualities is diconcerting.

I have some hesitation, however, in criticising an artist like Lautrec. I notice moreover that these rather uninteresting works were merely jobs done to order : two menus : *La Modiste* (1893) ; *The Modern Judgement of Paris* (1894) ; *An Invitation* (February 1895) ; *A Merry Christmas* (1896) ; an advertisement : *A la Maison d'Or* (1897) ; *New Year Greetings* (December 1897).

These may be taken, in the mass of Lautrec's lithographic work, as the equivalents of those trite phrases which an author of psychological novels cannot help inserting into dialogue ; things like « How are you? » or « Please take a seat », which a great stylist and pure poet would declare himself incapable of writing.

Apart from these funny sketches, his lithographic work is marvellously beautiful.

A drawing may represent a beautiful thing. With Lautrec the drawing is itself a beautiful thing, a separate entity, possessing a charm which makes you indifferent to the subject treated.

He only became interested in a subject because of some special characteristic or some particular arrangement of values, which he brought out vividly in his interpretation.

In *Slumber* (Plate XXXVII), one of the series of lithographs entitled *Elles*, he traces round the shoulders, the arms and the left breast, although full in the light, a line which obviously did not exist in the model. It is perfectly evident that he did not work literally from nature. So much the better ! He would never have conceived the bold idea of putting in that line attracting attention to the pretty inflexion of a curve, the line which says : « Look at this », or : « Print in heavy type. » It is like a newspaper headline, calling attention to the right thing. It is first-rate publicity.

Nonchalantly the line sweeps across the sheet. It knots and unknots and flows like a soft silk scarf : the central interest and « nœud » is the face of a young woman in bed (*Le petit déjeuner*) ; the open surfaces are the sheets or the legs swinging with the dragging bed-clothes (*Lassitude*) (Plate XXXVIII).

Such art has every appearance of brilliant improvisation. And it is improvisation in the sense that the sketches, and even the painted studies, by means of which Lautrec prepared each lithograph, were no longer in evidence when he came to draw on the stone. He had long since digested and assimilated them.

As far as he was concerned, these sketches and studies were exercises for the memory, not documents. By drawing them he learnt his subject by heart. This method enabled the actual execution to be carried out with all the unrehearsed charm and freshness of improvisation.

Lautrec, with his subject well prepared in his memory, used to draw his design with hand aloft, jauntily, singing all the time.

He possessed a vast repertoire of gallant old French songs and he enjoyed himself immensely singing them as he worked.

◨

There was always something boyish about Lautrec. In the Bibliothèque Nationale there are several proofs of *Marcelle Lender en buste* (1895, reduced plate), on which he has tried a light brown for the hair, a red for the hat and the flower in the bodice, and a green for the cloak. But this green ! It is as artless and glad as wash-tints done in safety colours... The proof without the framing line is delightful.

It is no bad compliment to say of an artist who is master of his craft, that his inspiration becomes one with the fresh imaginations of children. Musset is a poet of this type, Mozart a musician. Their fancy ranges free and for our greater pleasure. But, to their misfortune, they find it hard to submit to the ordinary conventions of life, those things which common wisdom accepts. They live more quickly than the ordinary run of men. Musset died at forty-seven, Mozart at thirty-five, Lautrec at thirty-six. He helped on his illness by over-indulgence in cocktails. In February 1899 mental trouble necessitated his confinement. He spent three months in a nursing-home, where a strict diet soon brought him round. His health had so far improved that at the end of this period of treatment he was able to resume work. In this nursing-home, he executed designs on lithographic stones, brought in by his publisher Stern, for two pictures to complete his illustration of the *Histoires naturelles*. In addition, he did twenty-two crayon drawings (Plate xxiv) representing circus scenes. He carried out all this work without models, only refreshing his memory of animals by taking a few walks round the Jardin d'Acclimatation. But his memory was prodigious. And he had so well observed clever dogs and performing horses, girl riders, Chocolat, Footit and Monsieur Loyal!

When he first returned home (May 17 1899), he behaved very well. He drank nothing but milk and even invited his friends to come and drink milk with him, as we see from *The Invitation*, dated May 15 1900 (Plate xl), in which the artist pictures himself standing by a cow and a magpie (la pie) which is looking up at the cow's... udder (le pis). Horrible pun!

This plate is a real document. Lautrec figures in it without flattery : short, stunted, with ill-shaped little legs. He has spurs at his heels, symbolic of his frustrated longing for an

active life in the open air ; on his head is a soft felt studio hat
with the brim turned down over his eyes.

His good behaviour did not last. He soon began drinking
again.

After this he only produced four more plates : a cover for
Jouets de Paris (1901), a book by his friend Paul Leclercq,
another for *Zamboula Polka*, a song composed by his cousin
Dihau, a lithograph *The Chestnut Seller* and a *Page of Sketches*,
which is of little consequence.

The Chestnut Seller might almost be called an Impressionist
landscape. It is seldom we come across such effects in Lautrec's work. The grey tone covering the whole page is certainly meant to represent the winter haze. A labourer trudges
by with his hands in his pockets. A woman is passing with her
fur collar turned up. The chestnut seller is seen raising the lid
of his oven.

Lautrec, sensitive to the perfumes of the seasons, was perhaps reminded by the reek of baked chestnuts of the good,
homely smell of a burnbake in the autumnal fields.

His feelings are softened. He is not the same man.

◼

As a lithographer, Lautrec at once found his bent. As a
painter, he hesitated all his life between spread colour and
hatching. In his application of the latter he was first of all
timid and unskilful. The portrait of his mother reading (1885,
Albi Museum, No. 53) is executed on canvas with small careful
strokes, betraying a vague Impressionist influence. In the
midst of this quilled furniture, these flower-spangled cur-
tains, by this table spread with a soft, rich cover, this white
marble fireplace, in this hushed family atmosphere, was there
insufficient stimulus for the painter? His treatment is mono-
tonous, his touch uniform.

Gradually he grew more confident. His hatching became broader and freer in compositions like the *Portrait of Mademoiselle Aline Gibert* (1887) ; *A Rest between two Waltzes* (Plate VII) ; *A la mie, au Moulin de la Galette : une nouvelle* (1891) ; *The Start of the Quadrille, Girls Waltzing* (1892).

In 1892, after executing the poster for the Moulin-Rouge, he tried colouring in shapes and produced *La Goulue entering the Moulin-Rouge* (Plate IX) and *A Table at the Moulin-Rouge* (Plate VIII). But in these cases, the shapes are not spread with full colour as in the small figures such as *Stout Maria* (1884) or *Carmen* (1885), *Rosa la Rouge* (1889) or *The Washerwoman* (1889), subjects simple enough to be modelled at a single application of colour. The complicated design of *La Goulue entering the Moulin-Rouge* and *A Table at the Moulin-Rouge* would have been lost under the pigment. So Lautrec worked up his effects in these pictures by means of separate lines of colour. Next, yielding to the charm of his own poster work, and seeking to obtain in painting as in lithography large coloured shapes, he closed up his hatching, made his strokes more and more alike in tone, and eventually so completely welded them together that in parts they offer a surface of uniform colour.

Nevertheless the strokes are still there. In places they shew through ; indeed, in many later paintings, they were not concealed at all. It must have been in 1886 or thereabouts that he saw the great pastels of Degas. In February 1893, he became acquainted with the artist. This was a signal for another bold breakaway.

By means of violent strokes, scarcely covering the ground, he recorded very vivid impressions : *In Bed* (1894, Albi Museum, No. 14) and *The Washerman* (1895, Albi Museum, No. 13) (Plate XII). In the latter work, however, the interest of the technique is quite outdone by the violence of the expression. Here Lautrec gave full play to his gift for bitter mockery and the representation of the base. The man is brin-

ging back the washing. He stoops with the weight of the
bundle. Unless, of course, he is bobbing before the mistress?
But it cannot be so. From his discontented look, at once
humble and rebellious, you would think he was a workman
about to put forward some claim. And that apache cap of
his! He surely has an open jack-knife up his sleeve. What
sort of place is he entering? What is this dim room with closed
shutters? Is he bringing a bundle of stolen goods for his
accomplice to conceal? The whole thing looks sinister.

What is the explanation of this? Is it the search for the
essence of character, or disappointed love, or kind feeling sti-
fled and thrust out of sight? The fact remains Lautrec chose
tainted creatures as his models. He frequented places of ill-
fame and portrayed their *habitués*.

He worked without respite, observing, scrutinising, dis-
secting.

This curiosity that nothing could escape, this passion for
drawing, that is to say this urgent need for self-expression,
was the reaction of a painfully sensitive and pent-up nature,
striving by every possible means to fight its way through to
liberty. Manifestations of art resulting from this driving force
are as full of pathos as a desperate attempt at escape from
captivity.

De profundis clamavi.

Lautrec descended into hell and portrayed the damned.
What he sought was character, and he found it where he
could.

He has executed on canvas, with very bright-toned hatching, an arresting work : *Monsieur et Madame* (1895, Albi
Museum, No. 18) (Plate XIII). These loathsome agents of vice
are held up for ever as repulsive beasts.

This painting is hallucinating. The woman's ugliness is
eloquent of tragic horror. And the style of the picture, glaring,
garish, loud, was only adopted to accentuate the impression
of disgust.

Is this really a picture? No, it is a caricature. It is a crayon drawing for an illustrated paper. — This is the most inferior type of work there is, and yet the caricature is a masterpiece. Lautrec took a liking to this sort of thing and produced in the following year half a dozen drawings for the « Rire ».

Frequently, by means of a few strokes of the brush in a single colour, he would give on a sheet of cardboard a brief suggestion of a movement or a character. In *Boneless Valentin and La Goulue at the Moulin de la Galette* (1888, Albi Museum, No. 57) the legs of the dancer appear actually in motion. In *M. Lucien Guitry and M*ⁱⁱᵉ *Marthe Brandes* (Albi Museum, No. 36) (Plate XI) the face without any forehead has a look of absolute bestiality.

These summary, yet final indications are dangerous examples. Young painters may think : « There is no need to go to much trouble. » But it takes a very clever artist successfully to realise a work of art with three strokes of the brush, or a very modest one to confess he is not capable of doing it.

The magnificent picture in the Toulouse Museum *A Woman Dressing* (1896, No. 618) (Plate XV) is merely a sketch on chamois paper. But what harmony there is between those three tones : the salmon pink of the hangings, the green of the screen and the ivory of the woman's back and arms, the whole supported by the strong black of her corsets and the more remote blacks of the hat and coat of the man who is sitting watching her !

The lower part of the picture contains nothing but a few streaks of colour indicating the train of the dress. This cunning negligence only serves to direct the attention to the upper part, where the pink, green and ivory sing together in delightful harmony.

I think this is a lovely painting, for the very reason that all its parts do not exercise an equal appeal to the eye. The interest is focussed here and rested there. It is an erroneous idea on the part of our western artists to think that the spectator's attention has to be held without respite. They weary it and send it to sleep. Lautrec, who knew a great deal about the Japanese and collected their engravings, learnt from their sparingly designed rectangles that the sensibility has to be rested, so that it may be refreshed and renewed.

He traced the summary lines and laid on the few tones in *A Woman Dressing* with such felicity and justness that the reproduction of the sketch in black and white wrongly gives it the appearance of an unfinished picture. Yet you would think the artist did it off-hand, in a playful mood. Well, you should see, in the portfolios in the Albi Museum, his drawings, the tracings of these drawings, the tracings of these tracings, and the tracings on which he has put a few touches of colour, the countless trials carried out for a single subject. And the picture in the Toulouse Museum is only a study, itself elaborated from another study (Albi Museum, No. 115), in turn made for a lithograph in the *Elles* series.

This picture is certainly not faultless. The tone of the shadow under the left forearm is false, making it appear dirty or gloved with grey. But a single fault does not destroy the beauty of a picture. The modelling of the back is a rare piece of specialised work. Rare, we must say, for Lautrec, for he seldom gave special treatment to any particular part. In the whole of his work I seem to recollect only one piece of modelling comparable with this back, that is the head of *M. Romain Coolus* (1899, Albi Museum, No. 138).

In the *Woman Dressing* Lautrec shewed himself more of a painter than he had ever been since his days at Cormon's studio, that is to say since the parting of the ways when, having to choose between drawing and painting, between the line and the pigment, between sketching and fine modelling, he embarked on a series of experiments which in the end led to nothing definite.

◧

With very great painters, the design, though it exists, is not felt.

You would think, for example, that Vermeer de Delft took the matter of his pictures so to speak bodily, and worked on it with complete freedom.

When you look at the portrait of the *Girl With A Flute* (Joseph Videner Collection, Philadelphia), it is unthinkable that the colours are based on an exact design on canvas. It is easier for me to think that those masses of light and shade moved over the panel, seeking their final position before gradually becoming fixed, in much the same way that molten matter cools down and solidifies. Lines! Of what use could they have been under that flow of lava? The idea seems as impossible as checking inspiration with dykes and ramparts, or driving a cyclone along rails!

Vermeer compounded his pigment with the raging appetite of a starving man chewing food. He realised effects akin to nature. He transformed matter. There was Manet, too, who painted with a loving hand small pictures of simple fruits. These diminutive works are miracles of sensuality. The representation is marvellous.

The painters who understood the appeal of these humble things and loved them were the hale and happy men such as Rembrandt, Vermeer, Chardin, Manet, who in their enthusiasm for pure painting did not strive to express through it ingenious ideas or illustrate witty sayings.

But Lautrec was not disposed merely to contemplate a Creation in which he felt he was so unkindly treated. He had a strong liking for all humorists.

It seems to me that true painters disdain to attract attention by representing the strange and the extraordinary; they strive before everything else for the exact tone, just as good writers prefer the correct word to the florid, emphatic expression. Corot is a great example of simplicity and truth of tone, and, for this reason, of strength.

When, by means of a very large composition, an artist wishes to sustain some thesis, the objects, or at least the rendering of their matter, becomes a secondary consideration.

The great Puvis de Chavannes used to keep Vilmorin's catalogues by him, and he actually took little flowers out of them with which to spangle the meadowlands of his great decorations.

Lautrec was no landscape painter. He kept to his studio, as Rembrandt, Vermeer and Chardin did, but not for the same reason. Rembrandt stayed for Saskia, Vermeer for Catherine and Chardin for Marguerite. All three have sung in their works the beauty of light streaming in through the casement, caressing a face, or a table, a plate, a glass, a chafing-dish, anything you like. They are happy, so everthing is beautiful. Lautrec remained in his studio because he could not do otherwise. He was always haunted by a strong desire to see the world. He came at a time of unsettled ideas. Even Manet, gifted as he was with a keen artistic appreciation of the most ordinary things, frequented noisy pleasure-haunts. He brought to them his powers of picturesque observation, and in *A Bar at the Folies-Bergère* all the inanimate things are admirably seen and realised. They are not, however, superior to his small paintings of fruit, pears, figs, lemons, etc. In fact I prefer the latter. His models lay to hand, and his realisation of them is very rich and beautiful. Nothing is more typical of a born painter than this kind of work. However, artists were beginning to be affected by the ferment of unrest. What this has resulted in today we know full well.

Chardin made do with his modest flat in the Rue Princesse, overlooking a murky yard, and there he painted gorgeous still-lives and his delightful scenes of domestic life. But your up-to-date twentieth-century artist must needs have a

mansion of his own in the neighbourhood of the Bois de Boulogne, which he only wants for part of the year. How indeed
can a well-to-do man stay at home in these days of easy travelling, with his luxurious limousine, his yacht, his private
airplane and Pullman cars to choose from?

When you have seen the Bay of Rio de Janeiro, how is it
possible to see beauty in a mere apple out of our orchards,
or in a rough earthenware jar, or even in a silver goblet?
Have you noticed the sort of subjects painters are choosing
today?

It seems to me that Chardin must have kept saying to
himself : « One day I may go blind and no longer be able to
see these fruits, this china and shining metal. » And so these
objects became all the more precious to him.

Speaking of all these familiar and homely things that sur-
round us, let me quote a few lines by the poet Charles Van
Lerberghe :

On went my bliss,
Singing 'mid lilies and roses,
Sought by my soul,
Who of her own blooms
Should have brought it to birth,
For I had but to list in quiet to hear it,
And lower my eyes to see.

Lautrec was restless and dissatisfied. He could never feel
comfortable at home.

When there is no woman to take charge, disorder invades
the house.

This careless and preoccupied batchelor, living alone, let
things go until he was literally submerged. Apart from canvases, frames, easels, stools, steps, etc., two large tables
encumbered the studio. One was laden with bottles, glasses,
shakers, all the apparatus necessary for mixing cocktails.
On the other were piled up pêle-mêle the sort of things artists

love to collect : dancers' slippers, periwigs, old books, autographs, vulgar photographs and precious Japanese prints. Lautrec even preserved an old door-knocker polished by use, the metal and design of which he thought magnificent.

Once a picture was begun, the charwoman was forbidden to touch any chair, draping or other accessory connected with it.

In the end Lautrec had just one little space among all this litter where he could sit and paint. So he was not very happy in his own place. The weakness of his legs often kept him indoors. Suddenly, one fine day, he felt he wanted a change of air. He packed his bag, a long, shallow, sausage-shaped thing made specially for him, so that it could be carried clear of the ground, and went off to Holland with Monsieur Maxime Dethomas. There he made a fairly rapid inspection of some of the museums and travelled a great deal on the canals.

He went on a voyage to Spain and Portugal on board the « Chili » with Monsieur Maurice Guibert, and brought back a sketch from which he later made a poster : *The Passenger aboard the 54 or a Trip on a Yacht* (1896).

Since 1890 he had been exhibiting at « La Libre Esthétique », occassioning periodic visits to Brussels.

Between 1895 and 1898 he went to London several times, where he was entertained by Whistler and chaperoned by Conder, the English Painter whom he portrayed at the table of the *Gens chic* (1893), in *The Box with the Golden Mask* (1893), and sitting beside the *Woman Dressing* (1896), the picture in the Toulouse Museum.

He preferred sea-voyages to railway journeys. To get to Taussat, on the Bassin d'Arcachon, or the Château de Malromé, he used to sail from Havre.

This restless soul, confined too often for his liking by his infirmity, never became reconciled to immobility, either in his life or in his craft.

There is a picture of his in the Toulouse Museum entitled

A Woman Frizzing her Hair. This sketch on cardboard shows a mass of reddish hair standing out from a green-tinted ground of very faint tone ; it trails away in a few streaks and patches of brown and salmon pink. The white camisole, touched with rainbow tints, recalling the shade of the ground, only exists in the upper part of the picture, for it fades below into the greyish brown board, with only a few markings to show the main folds.

◘

However, the practice of lithography was to provide a channel for this overweening desire for expression in clean line ; but, once satisfied, this desire lost its force. In the same year that he did the rough, multicoloured *Monsieur et Madame* (1895) (Plate XIII), Lautrec painted his fine *Portrait of M*^{me} *E. Pascal at the Piano* (Albi Museum, No. 49) (Plate XIV), putting into it his most patient and careful craftsmanship. It is a very elaborate portrait. In this case the hatching served only as preparatory work. The lines gradually brought up the final shade, which is sober and distinguished. Toward the end of his life Lautrec used separate lines less and less. By means of black and white washes and a few sober tones, he realised the fine, strong modelling of the portrait of his nursing-home attendant (1899, Albi Museum, No. 6) (Plate XVIII). In painting this, he seemed to pay little heed to method. He painted very simply, as he did in his early days, with greater knowledge and skill (for the portrait of his attendant is a finished work), but less colour : he thinned down his colours with turpentine and never employed again the opulent medley of pigments used in the *Gunner Saddling his horse* (1879).

He reverted occasionally to divided colour. In July 1899, in a moment of exasperation, he painted a picture bright enough to be composed of flower-petals : *The English Girl at the Star, at Havre* (Albi Museum, No. 47) (Plate XIX).

Then, in 1900, he painted the portrait of Monsieur Maurice Joyant sitting in a boat, with his gun held ready, in hard wild-fowling weather (Albi Museum, No. 50).

During the autumn and winter Lautrec used to spend week-ends with his oldest friend Monsieur Maurice Joyant shooting wild-fowl at Crotoy, at the mouth of the Somme. The two men, well wrapped up in waterproof coats, used to go out in a boat, M. Joyant to shoot at the birds as they came over, and Lautrec to observe and record the sportsman's movements.

This fine portrait is painted with plenty of turpentine. The tone of the waterproof coat in the gloom of this bitter wintry weather is marvellous. The sullen sky lours overhead. The attitude of the watchful sportsman is impressive. This was the artist's last masterpiece.

Right to the very end of his life, even when death was upon him, Lautrec was preoccupied with storing up visual impressions, with a view to constructing monuments of art. Travelling meant something more to him than the mere satisfaction of an idle man's curiosity. Every impression he received, every joy he experienced, he brought to the service of his Art, just as all men bring everything to the object of their constant thoughts and dreams : as the lover to the woman loved.

If Lautrec was ever in love, his affections were certainly never returned. His most tender lover was his painting. However, he was grateful to the woman who offered him, in the absence of affection, good comradeship.

Madame Le Margouin was the wife of one of his friends. She and Lautrec had characters which were closely akin. When they talked together, they were like children enjoying themselves. It must be recognised, in any case, that she meant no inspiration to him. The portrait he did of her in 1900 *La modiste* (Albi Museum, No. 51) is depressing. Lautrec is tired out, and this *modiste* looks anything but happy. She is gazing thoughtfully at her hands. She is posing, and that is quite sufficient to put any inspiration to flight. Lautrec's portrait of her is a very tame thing.

When, with a few strokes of the brush, he sketched in Boneless Valentin and la Goulue dancing together (1888, Albi Museum, No. 57), the legs were glaringly incorrect. Yet what does it matter? They express movement. Lautrec infused into his work the very elements of life : he caught the movement of birds in flight and men and women dancing.

' Late in the year 1900 he went to the theatre at Bordeaux and saw the opera *Messaline*. This gave him ideas for several paintings. In these the red dresses of the actresses shew bright against greenish-tinted scenery, with a thin neutral tone representing the boards underfoot.

In 1901, when the Doctor passed his final examination at the Faculty of Medecine, Lautrec grouped together in an academic composition the portraits of Doctors Fournier, Wurtz and Tapié de Celeyran. This sombre, rather dreary canvas, is in the Albi Museum (No. 41).

Lautrec was finished.

He had just spent three months in a nursing-home. He was placed under the supervision of an attendant, whose job was to prevent him frequenting bars. But he managed to get drinks in spite of the attendant. So, after a little while, feeling he was quite worn out, he sought quiet, first at Taussat, then at his mother's home, the Château de Malromé, where he died on September 9 1901.

After his death, a young woman acquainted with his family said : « I would gladly have taken care of Henri. I would have married him and prevented him drinking himself to death. » What a pity she did not do so ! But can we be sure that he would have managed to remain loyal, seeing his passing spasms for so many chance-met models?

One day he discovered a young chorus-girl who lived near by. She inspired a series of lithographs. This was *May Bel-*

fort. Then he became so infatuated with a barmaid at Havre that he broke his journey to stay with her. This was *The English Girl at the Star*. For the sake of the *Lady Travelling aboard the* 54, on the other hand, he went on to Lisbon. At the Moulin de la Galette and the Moulin-Rouge he was the regular painter of la Goulue. In these establishments and at the Jardin de Paris he was a constant follower of Jane Avril. In other night-haunts he was attentive to Cecy Loftus, Ida Heath, Lice Myrès...

His father was very indulgent over it all.

Some over-anxious friend said to him one day : « Henri is not leading a clean life. You ought to do something in the matter : he is bringing disgrace on the name. » « On our name ! » replied the Count, « Our name !... Poor little fellow ! We have to be thankful that he does not curse us for bringing him into the world as he is ! »

Lautrec never cursed his parents. Though he was sick, crippled and deformed, he knew magnificent joys, unrevealed by the episodes of his sad life, yet made plain to us by his works and unbroken effort. He lived in a dream-world, straining all his powers toward a rapturous ideal, beside which the realities of the workaday world are faint and insipid. Unfortunately the dream was stimulated by alcohol.

When he painted *Monsieur et Madame* his lower self was weltering in the depths. Yet all the time he was creating art, and from the filth in which his feet sank, his mind drew the virtue which brought forth those lovely blooms : *A Woman Dressing, Breakfast, Lassitude* and so many other beautiful works.

◘

I have tried to single out, in this life, the various events which had their effect upon the artist, and the influences which modified his Art, or at least his craft.

I see him as a boy of fifteen (1879) painting in bright, rich colours, as Guardi painted the view of Venice which is in the Albi Museum ; then, two years later, doing pictures of horses, in the manner of John Lewis Brown ; later on, in 1882, setting out portraits in a shy suggestion of the open air, in accordance with the formula of Bastien-Lepage.

I see him as an ardent draughtsman in the studios of Bonnat and Cormon, abandoning painting and discovering in the great pastels of Degas (those dating from 1885) a method which is at once painting and drawing, and which will free him from the tiresome operation of working colour between the lines of a complete and fixed design.

The art of poster-designing, in which he excels at his first attempt (1891), brings him back to a method, nearer true painting, of working in large coloured shapes, but does not definitely fix his line and leaves him hesitating.

I have attempted to assign him a place among painters. You must not expect from him the rich, harmonious effects of the Impressionists, nor yet the analyses of light realised by Degas in the *Rehearsal in the Dancers' Foyer* or *Le Pedicure*. Lautrec's best paintings are skilfully manipulated tones and shapes, the interplay of which is earnest, harsh, bitter, without any attempt at illusion.

Poster-designing leads him on to lithography. In this new craft, from 1893 onwards, he finds his true bent and produces his masterpieces. Quite at home in this kind of work, and happy to have discovered it, he casts off all his bitterness, and, as he celebrates true beauty, gives us a glimpse of unsuspected tenderness which establishes his kinship with Watteau.

BIBLIOGRAPHICAL NOTE

Studies published :

By Gustave Geffroy, in « La Justice » of February 19th. 1893, in « Le Journal » of January 14th. 1896, in « L'Humanité » of December 23rd. 1904 and in « La Gazette des Beaux-Arts » of August 1914 ;

By André Rivoire, in « La Revue de l'Art ancien et moderne » of December 1901 and April 1902 ;

By Arsène Alexandre, in « Le Figaro illustré », special April number 1902 and in « Les Arts » of August 1914 ;

By Gustave Coquiot, in « L'Art et les Artistes » of May 1914 ;

By Thadée Natanson, in « La Revue Blanche » of October Ist. 1901 ;

By André Rivoire, in « La Revue de l'Art ancien et moderne » of December 10th. 1901 and April 10th. 1902.

Books :

Esswein (Munich, 1912) ;
Louis Aubert, « Revue de Paris », 1910 : Harunobu et Toulouse-Lautrec ;
Gustave Coquiot (Paris, Blaizot, 1913 and Paris, Ollendorf, 1921) ;
Théodore Duret (Paris, Bernheim jeune, 1920) ;
Paul Leclercq (Paris, Floury, 1921) ;
Achille Astre (Paris, Floury, 1926) ;
Achille Astre (Paris, éditions Nilsson, 1926) ;
Maurice Joyant (Paris, Floury, 1926).

A complete set of the artist's engravings has been given by M. Loys in volumes X and XI of « Le Peintre-graveur au XIXe siècle ». All his paintings are reproduced at the end of « Toulouse-Lautrec » by M. Maurice Joyant.

I have only one further fact to add to the information supplied by these scholary works, that is that the monotype mentioned by Delteil (No. 338 *b*) is to be found in the « Musée de la Ville de Paris » (Petit-Palais).

PL. I.   ARTILLEUR SELLANT SON CHEVAL.
         ARTILLERYMAN SADDLING HIS HORSE.
         ARTILLERIST BEIM SATTELN SEINES PFERDES.
         ARTIGLIERE SELLANTE IL CAVALLO.
         ARTILLERO ENSILLADO SU CABALLO.

PL. 2. MAIL COACH. NICE.
MAIL COACH. NICE.
MAIL COACH. NIZZA.
MAIL COACH. NIZZA.
DILIGENCIA. NIZA.

PL. 3. UN TRAVAILLEUR A CELEYRAN.
A LABOURER AT CELEYRAN.
EIN ARBEITER IN CELEYRAN.
UN LAVORATORE A CELEYRAN.
UN TRABAJADOR EN CELEYRAN.

PL 4. LE JEUNE ROUTY A CELEYRAN.
YOUNG ROUTY AT CELEYRAN.
DER JUNGE ROUTY IN CELEYRAN.
IL GIOVANE ROUTY A CELEYRAN
EL JOVEN ROUTY EN CELEYRAN.

PL. 5. TÊTE DE FEMME DANS LE JARDIN DU PÈRE FOREST.
STUDY OF A WOMAN'S HEAD IN PÈRE FOREST'S GARDEN.
FRAUENKOPF IM GARTEN DES ALTEN FOREST.
TESTA DI DONNA NEL GIARDINO DEL PADRE FOREST.
GABEZA DE MUJER EN EL JARDIN DEL VIEJO FOREST.

PL. 7. REPOS ENTRE DEUX TOURS DE VALSE.
RESTING BETWEEN TWO WALTZES.
PAUSE ZWISCHEN ZWEI WALSERTOUREN.
SOSTA FRA DUE GIRI DI VALZER.
DESCANSO ENTRE DOS VUELTAS DE VALS.

PL. 8. UNE TABLE AU MOULIN-ROUGE.
A TABLE AT THE MOULIN-ROUGE.
EIN TISCH IM MOULIN-ROUGE.
UNA TAVOLA AL MOULIN-ROUGE.
UNA MESA DEL MOULIN-ROUGE.

PL. 9. LA GOULUE ENTRANT AU MOULIN-ROUGE.
THE DANCING GIRL « LA GOULUE » ENTERING THE MOULIN-ROUGE.
EINTRITT DER GOULUE IN MOULIN-ROUGE.
LA GOULUE ENTRANT NEL MOULIN-ROUGE.
LA GLOTONA ENTRANDO EN EL « MOULIN-ROUGE ».

PL. 10. PORTRAIT DE M. LOUIS PASCAL.
PORTRAIT OF Mr LOUIS PASCAL.
LOUIS PASCAL'S BILDNIS.
RITRATTO DEL S^re LUIGI PASCAL.
RETRATO DE M. LOUIS PASCAL.

PL. II. GUITRY ET BRANDÈS DANS « AMANTS ».
GUITRY AND BRANDÈS PLAYING IN « AMANTS ».
GUITRY UND DIE BRANDÈS IN « AMANTS ».
GUITRY E BRANDÈS NELLA COMMEDIA « AMANTS ».
GUITRY Y BRANDÈS EN « AMANTS ».

PL. 12. LE BLANCHISSEUR.
THE WASHERMAN.
DER WÄSCHER.
IL LAVANDAIO.
EL LAVADEERO

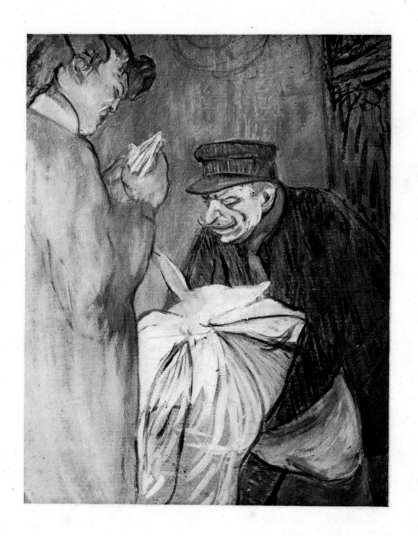

PL. 13. MONSIEUR ET MADAME.
MONSIEUR AND MADAME.
M^r ET Mme.
IL SIGNORE E LA SIGNORA.
SENOR ET SENORA.

PL. 14. PORTRAIT DE Mme E. PASCAL AU PIANO.
PORTRAIT OF Mrs E. PASCAL AT THE PIANO.
FRAU E. PASCAL AM KLAVIER.
RITRATTO DELLA SIGNORA E. PASCAL AL PIANOFORTE.
RETRATO DE Mme E. PASCAL AL PIANO.

PL. 15. FEMME A SA TOILETTE.
A WOMAN DRESSING.
FRAU AM PUTZTISCH.
DONNA ALLA TOELETTA.
MUJER HACIENDOSE LA « TOILETTE ».

PL. 16. DANSEUSE.
DANCER.
TÄNZERIN.
BALLERINA.
BAILARINA.

PL. 17. PORTRAIT DE M. HENRY NOCQ.
PORTRAIT OF Mr HENRY NOCQ.
HEINRICH NOCQ'S BILDNIS.
RITRATTO DEL Sr ENRICO NOCQ.
RETRATO DE M. HENRY NOCQ.

PL. 18. LE GARDIEN.
THE KEEPER.
DER HÜTER.
IL CUSTODE.
EL GUARDIAN.

PL. 20. CHOCOLAT DANSANT DANS LE BAR D'ACHILLE.
THE NEGRO CLOWN « CHOCOLAT » DANCING AT ACHILLE'S BAR.
CHOCOLAT TANZT IM BAR VON ACHILLE.
CHOCOLAT BALLANTE NEL BAR D'ACHILLE.
« CHOCOLATE DANZANTE » EN EL BARDE « ACHILLE ».

PL. 21. TÊTE DE FEMME DE PROFIL.
STUDY OF A WOMAN'S HEAD IN PROFILE.
FRAUENKOPF IM PROFIL.
CAPO DI DONNA DI PROFILO.
CABEZA DE MUJER VISTA DE PERFIL.

PL. 22. VENDANGES : RENTRÉE DE CHARS.
CARTS RETURNING FROM THE VINTAGE.
WEINLESE : HEIMKEHRENDE WAGEN.
VENDEMMIE : RITORNO DI CARRI.
VENDIMIAS : LLEGADO DE LOS CARROS.

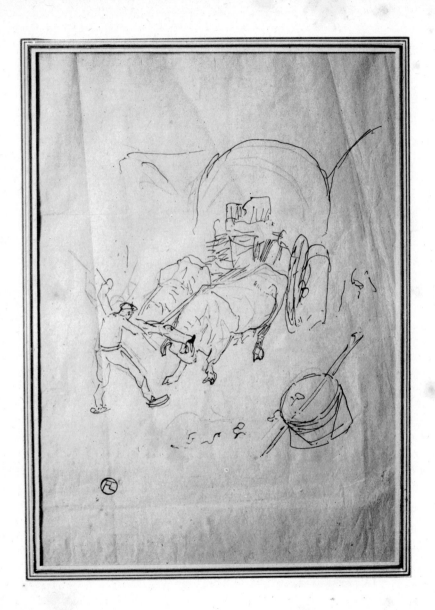

PL. 24. AU CIRQUE : FOOTIT.
        AT THE CIRCUS : THE CLOWN FOOTIT.
        IM ZIRKS : FOOTIT.
        NEL CIRCO : FOOTIT.
        EN EL CIRCO : FOOTIT.

PL. 27. FOLIES-BERGÈRE : LES PUDEURS DE M. PRUDHOMME.
AT THE FOLIES-BERGÈRE : LES PUDEURS DE M. PRUDHOMME.
FOLIES-BERGÈRE : DER VERSCHÄMTE HERR PRUDHOMME.
FOLIES-BERGÈRE : I PUDORI DI M. PRUDHOMME.
FOLIES-BERGÈRE : LOS PUDORES DE M. PRUDHOMME.

PL. 28. A L'OPÉRA : Mme ROSE CARON DANS « FAUST ».
AT THE OPÉRA : Mrs ROSE CARON IN « FAUST ».
IM OPERNHAUS : FRAU ROSE CARON IM « FAUST ».
NEL'OPERA : LA SIG^ra ROSA CARON NEL « FAUST ».
EN LA OPERA : Mme ROSE CARON EN « FAUSTO ».

PL. 29. RÉJANE ET GALIPAUX.
RÉJANE AND GALIPAUX.
RÉJANE UND GALIPAUX.
RÉJANE E GALIPAUX.
RÉJANE Y GALIPAUX.

PL. 32. YVETTE GUILBERT. (PROFIL A DROITE).
　　　　YVETTE GUILBERT. (RIGHT-HAND PROFILE).
　　　　YVETTE GUILBERT. (PROFIL RECHTS).
　　　　IVETTA GUILBERT. (PROFILO DA DIRITTO).
　　　　YVETTE GUILBERT. (PERFIL DEL LADO DERECHO).

PL. 35. LENDER ET AUGUEZ CHANTANT LA CHANSON DE FORTUNIO.
Mlles LENDER AND AUGUEZ SINGING FORTUNIO'S SONG.
LENDER UND AUGUEZ SINGEN FORTUNIO'S LIED.
LENDER E AUGUEZ CANTANTI LA CANZONE DI FORTUNIO.
LENDER Y AUGUEZ CANTANDO LA CANCION DE FORTUNIO.

PL. 37. LE SOMMEIL.
SLEEP.
DER SCHLAF.
IL SONNO.
EL SUENO.

PL. 38. ELLES : LASSITUDE.
      SHES : WEARINESS.
      SIE : MÜDIGKEIT.
      ESSE : STANCHEZZA.
      ELLAS : LASITUD.

PL. 39. LA GRANDE LOGE.
THE STAGE BOX.
DIE GROSZE LOGE.
LA GRANDE LOGGIA.
EL GRAN PALCO.

PL. 40. INVITATION A UNE TASSE DE LAIT.
THE CUP OF MILK.
EINLADUNG ZU EINER TASSE MILCH.
INVITAZIONE AD UNA TASSA DI LATTE.
INVITACION A UNA TAZA DE LECHE.

5 avenue Frochot

Henri de Toulouse-Lautrec sera très fâché si vous voulez
bien accepter un tasse de lait le Samedi 15 Mai
vers 3 heures et demie après midi